Go[illegible]l the Church

Encouraging a Biblical Vision of Fatherhood

Peter Munce

Curate-assistant

GROVE BOOKS LIMITED
RIDLEY HALL RD CAMBRIDGE CB3 9HU

Contents

Acknowledgments

I would like to express my thanks to a number of people who have helped with the publication of this booklet. First to my tutor at the Church of Ireland Theological Institute who supervised my dissertation, the Revd Dr Paddy McGlinchey. I would also like to thank the Revd Dr Robin Stockitt for encouraging me to pursue this topic within the Grove series. I thank the Revd William Orr for his information about ministry in Muckamore Parish. I also thank the Revd Andrew Sweeney and the Revd Joanne Megarrell who have supported research on this topic during my year as a deacon in Ballymoney and as a curate in Moira.

I thank the Lord Jesus Christ for his loving kindness and grace in my life and for the gift of my wife and children. This book is dedicated to my loving and patient wife Celia and our three children—Olivia, Joseph and Eliza—who have taught me the most about what it means to be a dad. Soli Dei Gloria!

First Impression June 2017
ISSN 0144-171X
ISBN 978 1 78827 013 7

1 Introduction

Picture the scene. You are a dad with three kids. It is 3am and your wife is settling your newborn baby. Meanwhile, your four year old has just wet the bed and your six year old is up being sick with a tummy bug. If you are anything like me, before you rise from your broken slumber the thought running round your head might be this: 'No-one ever told me fatherhood would be like this…!' Yet, is there anything more rewarding and frustrating, exciting and challenging than being a dad? It is the adventure of a lifetime. This book is about being a dad and how the church can help to equip dads with the tools they need to live out a biblical vision of fatherhood. It encourages the church to take seriously the need to engage dads as part of the prophetic call in the Book of Malachi, of turning 'the hearts of fathers to their children and the hearts of children to their fathers' (Mal 4.5–6).

In recent years, society and culture have been busy reflecting on what it means to be a dad in twenty-first century Britain. From the nation's obsession with Prince William's ability to deal with baby George's car seat when leaving hospital for the first time, to Daddy Pig in *Peppa Pig,* to Pete Brockman (the dad from the popular BBC series *Outnumbered*), we are not short of social and cultural representations of fatherhood.

Indeed, family life in our twenty-first century postmodern culture is on a very interesting journey—the destination of which is unknown. The dizzying pace of technological, sociocultural and economic change has placed unprecedented pressures on the family unit to such an extent that family life has been challenged and undermined in ways that would have been unthinkable in previous generations. One of the consequences of these changes is that our understanding of what constitutes the family unit has been called into question. A family with one father and one mother is no longer normative. This has left fatherhood in a state of flux as, together with wider society, men ask what it means to be a father in this complex world in which we live.

Our understanding of what constitutes the family unit has been called into question

Amid these changes stands the church, which is called to proclaim the gospel of Jesus Christ. At the heart of this good news of the Christian faith is the revelation of the Father's love in the sending of his Son for the salvation of the world so that, as John's gospel puts it, 'Everyone who believes in him may not perish but may have eternal life' (John 3:16). According to J I Packer, '...you sum up the whole of New Testament teaching in a single phrase, if you speak of it as a revelation of the fatherhood of the holy creator.'[1] The Christian faith, therefore, has much to say about fatherhood, not just from a theological perspective, but also in seeking to answer the question of what it means to be a father in the complex cultural landscape of our postmodern age.

This booklet aspires to be a fresh word on the subject of fatherhood in the Bible

This booklet aspires to be a fresh word on the subject of fatherhood in the Bible and aims to do three things. *First,* it seeks to explore what culture and society have to say about fatherhood—cultural exegesis, if you like. This is a vital task the church must undertake before it begins to engage with this issue. As Kevin Vanhoozer states, 'Only when we truly understand what is happening around us can we [the church] engage our world intelligently and effectively (and evangelistically).'[2] *Secondly,* it wants to help both dads and the church to think much more deeply about what a biblical theology of fatherhood looks like. *Thirdly,* it aims to explore how the local church can reach out to and work with dads in their church and local community.

Its genesis springs from three overlapping sources. First, I am blessed by the Lord to be a father to three amazing children. As I write this I am constantly seeking to discover for myself what it means to be a godly, Christlike and Spirit-filled father to them. I praise God for them because they have taught me more about what it means to be a man, a husband, a father and a follower of Jesus Christ than anyone. Secondly, it emerges from my own experience of pastoral ministry within the Church of Ireland. Thirdly, the booklet has emerged from research that was first undertaken for the author's Masters in Theological Studies (MTh) dissertation for ordination in the Church of Ireland.

The Face of Contemporary Fatherhood

2

This chapter explores the two deep-running trends that lie at the heart of social and cultural representations of fatherhood today: 'father absence' and 'father involvement.' Put differently, contemporary fatherhood is driven by the paradox that just as more fathers become intimately involved in the lives of their children, fathers in other parts of society are either walking away from their fatherly responsibilities of their own volition or because of complex familial circumstances. Nowhere do we see these two faces of contemporary fatherhood more clearly than on our TV screens. Two Channel 4 programmes illustrate this perfectly: *One Born Every Minute* and *Shameless*.

Sixty years ago men were largely absent from childbirth. Fast-forward to 2017 and all that has changed. *One Born Every Minute* is a fly-on-the-wall reality TV documentary based in maternity wards across the UK. One of the most striking things about the programme is the reaction of the men. Most men do not know what to do at childbirth, but would not miss it for the world; then, when the baby appears, the tears come. *One Born Every Minute* shows fathers at their most vulnerable and highlights how they want to be intimately involved in the lives of their newborn children. *Shameless* tells the story of life in Chatsworth, a fictional Manchester council estate. Its principal character is an alcoholic father called Frank Gallagher. *Shameless* depicts fatherlessness, broken father-children relationships and reflects the failure and complexity of fatherhood in twenty-first century Britain.

Fatherless Britain

In twenty-first century Britain the reality is that we live in an increasingly fatherless society. This is evidenced by the increasing number of children growing up in lone-parent families and in the growing trend of absent fathers. According to estimates by the Office for National Statistics (ONS) there were just over three million lone-parent families in the United Kingdom in 2015. Of these three million lone-parent families, over 2.5 million are lone-mother families.[3] According to the same ONS data, almost four million children in Britain live without their father at home.[4] Significantly, research by the Centre for Social Justice (CSJ), has highlighted the extent of fatherlessness in Britain. In their report 'Fractured Families' they estimate that around one million children

We live in an increasingly fatherless society

have no meaningful contact with their fathers.[5] Supporting this assertion, the think tank, the Fatherhood Institute,[6] estimates that 'somewhere between one and two million children in the UK at any one time, are not in meaningful contact with their father.'[7] As the CSJ points out, 'The proportion of families with dependent children headed by lone parents has increased from 8 per cent in 1971 to 22 per cent in 2014.[8] The CSJ have further suggested, through their research, that in Britain:

> It is therefore highly concerning that over a million children have no meaningful contact with their fathers and by the end of their childhood a young person is considerably more likely to have a smartphone than a resident father: only 57 per cent of 15 year olds are still living with their fathers while 62 per cent own a smartphone.[9]

These startling statistics highlight the extent of fatherlessness in Britain today. However, fatherlessness is just one face of contemporary fatherhood in Britain. Alongside the story of fatherless Britain is another story—this time of fathers who long for a more involved relationship with their children. At its core, it captures the idea that men see their role as fathers as representing something more than simply financial provision. Furthermore, many millennial fathers, affected by the way they were fathered, changes in gender roles and the greater number of women in the labour market, have embraced greater involvement with their children as a key part of their fatherly responsibilities.

The 'New Fatherhood'

Today, social media is awash with celebrity fathers sharing pictures of themselves and their children. Indeed, when the CEO of Facebook, Mark Zuckerberg, announced that he was taking two months' paternity leave he was lauded as having 'changed the face of fatherhood.'[10] When Prince William appeared on TV screens after the birth of his first child, carrying the newborn Prince George out of hospital and placing him into his car seat, he was praised for his fresh approach to fathering. What these cultural reference points neatly encapsulate is the idea of the 'new fatherhood.'

What is meant, then, by 'new fatherhood'? As a cultural ideal, new fatherhood emerged in the 1980s to describe a new kind of dad who was more likely to be actively involved in the life of their children and more demonstrably caring and nurturing as a father. Two of the UK's leading sociologists of fatherhood, Esther Dermott and Tina Miller, argue that '...the language of "involved" or "intimate" fatherhood has become more commonplace, normative, even'[11] in the cultural characterization of fatherhood in twenty-first century Britain.[12]

To help us unpack further what is meant by this new idea of fatherhood let us look at four key areas.

1 Expectation for Fathers to Provide Financially and Also Be Involved as Parents

First, it is important to note that, despite the importance now attached to new fatherhood, contemporary fathers and fathering practices are still often defined and influenced by the idea of the father as the breadwinner and provider for the family. Tina Miller argues that, despite the contemporary emphasis on new fatherhood, 'paid work remains a significant factor' in terms of men's self-understanding of their role as fathers. Put differently, in contemporary society, the cultural expectation is that fathers are expected both to provide financially and also to be intimately involved in the lives of their children.[13]

2 Opening Up of the Labour Market

The second observation we can make is that the increase of new fatherhood can also be attributed to the opening up of the labour market to greater numbers of women. This makes new fatherhood as much the product of an increase of dual-income domestic earning as anything. Men are no longer the sole breadwinners or capable of fulfilling such a role. Moreover, because of this, the old division of labour of the mother providing care, nurture and staying at home whilst the father goes out to work has had to be radically reconsidered. Increasingly, both parents have to work to support the family financially. Indeed, irrespective of whether fathers have liked it or not, to keep daily family life functioning well, they have had to become more involved in aspects of parental care and provision that were previously more associated with mothers.

3 Father Involvement is an Intentional Choice

Thirdly, for other fathers, greater involvement in their child's life is an intentional choice. Many fathers from the so-called millennial generation have chosen to be closely involved in the lives of their children. According to research conducted by the British organization, 'Working Families,' 'Millennial parents (aged 16–35) are more likely to both work full-time, flexibly, and share caring responsibilities.'[14] In part, this generation is driven by a desire to father their own children differently from the way they were fathered by a distant or absent dad. Their experience is neatly encapsulated in the Harry Chapin song, *Cat's in the Cradle,* about a father who, because of work and the need to provide for his family, is too busy to spend time with his son. The dad buys his son a baseball for his birthday, but is too busy to play with his children. For many fathers, this is heartbreaking. There is a desire to spend time with their children but the reality is that bills need to be paid and the family provided for. Many millennial fathers, therefore, are seeking to father differently from how they were fathered.

4 Rise of the 'Stay-at-home' Dad

Fourthly, in Britain, changes in culture and in government policy also saw new fatherhood evolve into something more than just the emotional and practical involvement of a father in their child's life, with the rise of a new phenomenon known as the stay-at-home dad. In 1997 the new Labour government introduced paid statutory paternity leave for fathers and in 2015 new legislation from the coalition government allowed parents to share between them statutory maternity leave, allowing the mother to return to work early and allowing the father to provide childcare. Furthermore, changes in the labour market have meant that quite often the woman earns more than the man, meaning that many families have made the decision for the husband to stay at home whilst the wife goes out to work.

3

Calling God Father

At the centre of Christian worship, doctrine and practice is a belief in the triune God: Father, Son and Holy Spirit. Since the fourth century, the central credal confession of the Christian church has begun with these words, 'We believe in one God, the Father, the Almighty, maker of heaven and earth, of all that is, seen and unseen.'[15] These words find their basis in what has been referred to as a Christian version of the central credal proclamation of Israel's faith—the *Shema Yisrael* (Deut 6.4)—in 1 Cor 8.6: 'For us there is one God, the Father, from whom are all things and for whom we exist…' In this chapter we explore why we call God Father and how that important confession lies at the centre of our Christian faith. We also look at what God's Fatherhood looks like through the Parable of the Prodigal Son (Luke 15.11–32).

God as Father in the Old Testament

The references to the fatherhood of God in the Old Testament are easily overlooked and yet the promises made by the LORD to Israel are the foundation for the New Testament's confession of God as Father.[16] The idea of God as father, whilst not as prominent, was not unfamiliar in the Old Testament. In terms of the Old Testament we can understand God's fatherhood in relation to the election of Israel as the LORD's 'firstborn son' (Exod 4.22). Furthermore, in the Old Testament the LORD is often referred to as a 'Father to the fatherless' and acts with fatherly goodness as a protector of the vulnerable (Ps 68.5). Indeed, there is rich biblical material that exists, particularly within the Hebrew Scriptures, on God's radical concern for orphans or the fatherless. In most instances where *orphan* appears in the Hebrew Scriptures it does so alongside widows and sojourners as being of particular concern to the LORD and deserving of the protection of the community of faith. This 'vulnerable triumvirate,' as Walter Brueggemann describes them, are mentioned at various points in the Old Testament (Deut 10.18; 14.29; 16.11, 14; 24.17–21; Ps 94.6; 146.9; Jer 7.6; 22.3; Zech 7.10).[17] We can summarize this material by saying: concern for the fatherless and the orphan is rooted in the very nature and character of the LORD, whose covenant people are called to mirror the intensity of the LORD's concern for this group of vulnerable persons.

God as Father in the New Testament

Names are important. I remember the long debates my wife and I had about naming our children. As a new curate in a busy parish, I have to work extremely hard to remember everybody's name. In the Bible there are many names by which God is known. However, as we read through the gospel narratives it becomes clear that 'Father' was how Jesus chose to address God. Just as Israel was the Lord's firstborn son, now Jesus, as the true Israel, is God's only Son given in love by the Father for the salvation of the world (John 3.16). According to Tom Smail, there are 245 occasions in the New Testament when God is called 'Father.' The majority of these occurrences in the New Testament can be found in the Gospel of John and here, as elsewhere in the NT, where the word appears it does so most often on the lips of Jesus.[18]

It must be recognized that in the late twentieth century calling God, 'Father' has come under unprecedented pressure from feminist theology, which argues that calling God Father is sexist and only serves to legitimate patriarchy and denigrate the role of women in the church. As a consequence, there have been attempts to introduce gender-inclusive liturgy, moves to call God 'Mother' or to replace God the Father with gender-neutral terms such as 'parent' or 'creator.' However, to call God 'Mother' rather than Father not only plays fast and loose with the biblical witness to the first person of the Trinity but also marks a departure from the orthodox, credal confession of the church. To further consider the question of why Christians call God 'Father' it is helpful to consider the words of Emil Brunner:

> Our God is called the 'Father in heaven.' This is the name, which the Christian church gave him from the very beginning. The fact, however, that she gave him this name was not her own discovery, nor was it due to her own caprice. It was taught by the Son, by Jesus Christ. The fact that Jesus Christ is the Son…not a son alongside of other sons or children of God is the decisive central confession of faith of the primitive Christian church.[19]

It is significant that each time Jesus is recorded as praying to God in the gospels, with the exception of the cry of dereliction on the cross, the address is to God as Father (Mark 15.34). Furthermore, on the three occasions where *Abba* appears in the New Testament (Mark 14.36; Rom 8.15; Gal 4.6), it is in the context of what Kenneth Bailey describes as 'fervent prayers.'[20] This reminds us that, ultimately, Jesus' address to God as Father is not just an important theological doctrine central to the Christian faith, but is also an invitation to his disciples, through prayer, to enter into an intimate encounter with the God and Father of our Lord Jesus Christ. When Jesus prays '*Abba* Father' in the Garden of Gethsemane he uses familial language, which illustrates for us the closeness and intimacy of this relationship (Mark 14.36). Indeed, the good news at the heart of the Christian faith is that through Jesus and the power of the Spirit we can become children of God (Rom 8.15; Gal 4.6).

Adoption is a powerful New Testament metaphor for salvation. As John puts it in the prologue to his gospel: 'To all who believed him and accepted him, he gave the right to become children of God' (John 1.12). God the Father—the one who is the 'maker of heaven and earth, of all that is seen and unseen' is also a good Father who is intimately interested in his children. When Jesus calls God Father, therefore, he invites his followers to do the same and to enter into a relationship of worship and devotion.

God's Fatherhood and Human Fatherhood

The approach this booklet takes to the relationship between God's fatherhood and human fatherhood is that God's fatherhood provides a 'Divine Critique' of human fatherhood.[21] In other words, God's fatherhood is the standard against which all human fatherhood is measured.

In our church pews there are many men and women who carry a father hunger deep in their hearts because of absent, abusive or apathetic fathers. For these people, and because of their broken father relationship, the idea of a heavenly Father who loves them is a complete anathema. However, we must understand that it is not from our own experience of human fatherhood, whether it is good or bad, abusive, absent or apathetic or even celebrated, that we understand God's fatherly goodness. We do not project our earthly idea or experience of human fatherhood onto our understanding of God's fatherhood. Karl Barth put it like this: 'We must not measure by natural human fatherhood what it means that God is our Father. It is from God's fatherhood that our natural human fatherhood acquires any meaning and dignity.'[22] Similarly John Stott argues that 'The true relation between human fatherhood and the divine fatherhood is neither one of analogy…nor one of projection…but rather one of derivation (God's fatherhood being the archetypal reality).'[23] Indeed, as Walter Brueggemann reminds us, God's fatherhood is so often presented in Scripture as a 'counter image to much of what is known, anciently and contemporarily about fathers.'[24]

We do not project our earthly idea of human fatherhood onto our understanding of God's fatherhood

There is not enough space in this short book to do justice to or to explore all the ways in which the triune God might act as the pattern for human parenting. Suffice it to say that the sustaining love of God the Father, the sacrificial living and compassion of his Son our Lord Jesus Christ and the intimacy brought by the sending of the Spirit provide the standard against which all earthly fathers, indeed all parenting, can be measured.

There are different ways in which we could further explore and unpack what God's fatherhood and fatherly character looks like. One way is by looking of the parable of the Prodigal Son in Luke's gospel (Luke 15.11–28). Jesus defines *Abba*—the fatherhood of God—not as an ancient Near Eastern patriarch but as a loving Father full of compassion and goodness. Kenneth Bailey argues that:

> In the famous parable of the prodigal son, Jesus is best understood to be defining the word father for the use he intends to make of it. In that story Jesus breaks all bounds of human patriarchy and presents an image of a father that goes beyond anything his culture expected from any human father, as we will see. He was not describing fathers as he knew them but rather creating a new image that he intended to use as a model for God.[25]

Jesus, relying upon the example of a human father, gives us the image of God's fatherhood as gracious, loving, compassionate and kind. The father who runs endures shame and embarrassment, yet shows nothing but costly, compassionate love—this is the divine critique of all earthly fatherhood. This is the Father who moves first. In the parable of the Prodigal Son Jesus reveals something of the character of God, which is both a powerful critique of and also a standard against which all earthly fathers (and mothers) can be measured. According to Bailey, in this parable, 'The image of God as a compassionate father is given its finest definition in all of Scripture.'[26]

The actions of the father towards both sons in this parable are astonishing, especially when one considers how a traditional patriarch in the culture of the time would have been expected to act. It is worth reflecting on some ways in which the father in this parable confounds patriarchy in the culture at the time. First, in his response to the younger son's initial request. The younger son approaches his father and asks for his share of the father's estate. The son wants his share whilst the father is still alive. In effect what he is really saying is, 'I want you dead.'[27] Both the request and the father's response are equally astounding and so, from the outset of this parable, it is clear that Jesus is not talking about a traditional patriarch of the culture of the time.

Secondly, after squandering his wealth in a distant land the younger son risks ceremonial uncleanness by his association with pigs (forbidden under Jewish law). Hungry, desolate and in despair he comes to his senses and returns to the father. The father sees him at a great distance, has compassion, runs towards him and kisses him (Luke 15.20). This is far removed from how his culture would have expected him to act. Jesus presents this father as loving and compassionate—a father who has been watching a track leading into the horizon in this village waiting for his younger son to return.

Thirdly, this father not only receives the younger son back—he runs to greet him.[28] Here we see a meeting point between Greek and Semitic culture—both of which adhere to the principle that 'People of prominence did not and do not run in public.'[29] For the father to run in public towards his son like this is deeply humiliating in the world of Jesus' parable. However, for the father this cost is worth paying as he seeks to embrace and restore his lost son.

Fourthly, through the action of the elder brother, we can also understand how Jesus subverts the patriarchal image of a father of the culture of the time. Indeed, the older brother, in his angry lecture of the father because of his response to the return of the younger brother, shows that he has no more respect for his father than his younger brother. However, when confronted with the elder son's anger, the father, once again, demonstrates his loving nature and compassionate character. The insult and insolence of the elder son in refusing to take his place at the father's side was a deep violation of custom and relationship (Luke 15.28). As with the younger son, the father would have been well within his rights to rebuke and punish the son. However, the father humbles himself and comes outside to 'plead' with him.[30] The father treats both sons with equal tenderness, love and care. Indeed, the father's equal treatment of his sons in this parable provides a powerful challenge to dads today to think of the ways in which we might be tempted to treat our children differently. The reasons for this will be many and varied, but one thing this parable teaches dads is to show no favouritism either explicitly or implicitly towards their children.

We see, therefore, that the parable of the Prodigal Son functions as the ultimate illustration of what is meant by the divine critique of human fatherhood. Moreover, when Jesus was choosing an earthly father to symbolize what he meant by calling God Father, he chose not a dominating, oppressive patriarchal figure from the culture of the time. Instead, Jesus chose the image of a loving, compassionate, kind father as a symbol of what the *Abba* to whom he prayed looked like. Mindful of this discussion, if God's fatherhood is the standard by which human fatherhood is measured, we now turn to consider the picture the Bible paints of human fatherhood.

4 What Does the Bible Say About Being a Dad?

Culture and society have much to say about what it means to be a dad but what does the Bible have to teach us about this? We argue here that the biblical vision for fatherhood is of father-involved families where fathers take the initiative in showing love to their children, acting self-sacrificially, and where fathers are intimately involved in the lives of their children and families.

What Do Ephesians and Colossians Say About Being a Dad?

In the New Testament, fathers are addressed directly in two passages (Eph 6.4 and Col 3.21). On first reading of these biblical texts, such instructions appear to be very specifically about the father's role in bringing children up in the Christian faith and about not provoking or exasperating their children. However, when one uncovers something of the cultural context in which these texts were written their meaning becomes much more powerful and broader in scope than it might appear. The *patria potestas*—the absolute legal powers that the father had over children—are a well-known feature of Greco-Roman society in the early first century. In particular, as Dionysius of Halicarnassus reminds us, this *patria potestas* allowed the father significant power over his children, including the capacity to, 'imprison him, to scourge him, to put him in chains, and keep him at work in the fields, or to put him to death.'[31] In short, the *patria potestas* meant fathers had absolute power and authority over children in their household.

Mindful of this cultural background to the text, the significance of what Paul has to say to fathers becomes much clearer. Rather than emphasize the authority, power and rule that a Greco-Roman father would have over their children, these texts invite the father, 'to be gentle, patient educators of their children, whose chief weapon is Christian instruction, focused on loyalty to Christ as Lord.'[32] Whilst the authority that fathers had over their children is 'assumed in the call to children to obey their parents' it is still significant that neither instruction to the father makes explicit reference to their power.[33] Further still, what these passages arguably envisage is a reciprocal relationship between a father and his children. On the one hand, children are called to obey their parents, with a reminder of the fifth commandment to honour your father and mother (Eph 6.1–3; Col 3.20) and on the other hand, fathers are called not to exasperate their children (Eph 6.4) or provoke them (Col 3.21). In this sense, in Eph 6.4 Paul 'does not exhort fathers to exercise authority';[34] neither does he presuppose that children are merely the property of the father 'over whom the father has legal rights.'[35] Instead, this passage (along with passages such as Mark 10.13–15) makes clear that children are 'owed dignity as human beings in their own right.'[36]

Moreover, because of the preceding discussion, it is possible to argue that what these passages suggest is that the Christian picture of fatherhood stands in contrast to Greco-Roman culture and society at the time. The Christian father is to be neither the *patria potestas* nor the Greco-Roman patriarch, but rather the servant leader following the way of Christ as Eph 5.19–33 reminds us. This passage calls on husbands to 'love their wives just as Christ loved the church and gave himself up for her' (Eph 5.25). This suggests that husbands (and fathers) are to love their family as Christ loved the church, which includes the possibility that we may be called, literally, to lay our lives down for our families. In reality, the practical outworking of Paul's exhortation is that men, as husbands and fathers, put their family's needs and interests above their own. They live sacrificially in terms of money, time and care. Laying your life down for your family does not in all cases mean the loss of your life physically but the call to prioritize the needs of your family above your own.

> **The practical outworking of Paul's exhortation is that men put their family's needs and interests above their own**

The Role of the Dad in Passing on Christian Faith in the Home

One of the central and most important responsibilities the Bible ascribes to fathers is in the passing on of faith to their children. This is very clearly stated in the second half of Eph 6.4, which instructs fathers to bring their children up 'in the training and instruction of the Lord.' However, we begin our examination not in the Ephesians passage we have just considered, but in the Hebrew Scriptures, where the father's role in the passing on of faith first emerges as a key fatherly responsibility.

The family in ancient Israel served as a 'vehicle of continuity for the faith, history, law and traditions of the nation' and the 'preservation of these national assets lay in the hands of the father especially.'[37] This idea of teaching children and instructing them in faith recurs throughout the Hebrew Scriptures. Beginning in Deuteronomy, the deuteronomist connects the obedience of the LORD's commands with the instruction and passing on to children of religious ordinances in the home. The father's role in instruction was to teach the law to children (Deut 11.19) and talk about it in the home (Deut 6.7). He is to teach his children and give explanations to them, 'concerning particular events, institutions, or memorials' that were central to the faith of Israel.[38]

This theme of the family's role in passing on faith is also seen in the wisdom literature of Psalms and Proverbs (Ps 78.5–7 and Prov 22.6). From these two passages a number of points can be made. First, the commands and decrees of the LORD are to be taught, not kept silent. They are to be proclaimed from one generation to the next. Secondly, this is not done as an empty gesture without meaning and purpose, but rather that future generations may know them. Thirdly, this pattern was to occur not just once but to be repeated in successive generations. Fourthly, this act of passing on faith—by teaching and instruction—was about remembrance of what the LORD has done for the people of Israel and ensuring obedience to his commands, so that ultimately people's hope would be put in God. Moreover, with this foundation in place, the expectation was that if children were grounded in the LORD's decrees, ordnances and commands they would have an enduring faith that would last. The trajectory, therefore, of Deuteronomy and the wisdom literature points to the New Testament and Paul's exhortation in Ephesians to bring up children 'in the training and instruction of the Lord.'

To Summarize—the Biblical Vision of Fatherhood

To summarize, then, it can be argued that the Bible emphasizes high paternal involvement in the life of children through care, love and attention. In the previous chapter we saw how the father in Jesus' Parable of the Prodigal Son showed generous, compassionate and unconditional love to both sons, who because of their actions deserved to be treated in the opposite way to how their father acted. It is possible to argue that the example of this compassionate, loving father, who acts sacrificially towards his children, is reinforced by the instructions for fathers contained in Ephesians and Colossians. Furthermore, if passing on the faith to their children is one of the father's primary tasks, then that presumes the existence of a close relationship between father and child. Just as God the Father is not a distant father, but is involved in every aspect of our lives, so earthly fathers are also called to be intimately involved in their children's lives. The father is called not to act as a distant patriarch, but as an involved, loving, compassionate and self-sacrificial father who, in leading his family, puts their interests first.

Earthly fathers are called to be intimately involved in their children's lives

Ideas for Engaging Dads with God and the Church

5

In this final chapter we will look at what the priorities might be for a local church seeking to engage with dads in the local community. We will also explore some ideas that churches might want to use to help with this work because the local church has a vital role to play in helping men be fathers.

Priority Areas to Think About

Help Men Pass On Their Christian Faith in the Home

In the previous chapter we explored the fact that one of the key responsibilities of biblical fatherhood is the command to raise children in the Christian faith. Yet this role is, arguably, one of the most often overlooked. A central priority for any local church must be to help dads do this. Over the past ten years, academic research has demonstrated the crucial role that families, and specifically fathers, have to play in the transmission of faith to their children. Indeed, despite the prevailing cultural narrative, which suggests the marginalization of parental influence over children, especially teenagers, this research has emphasized the important role of parents in the transmission of faith.[39] It is worth reflecting briefly on these two pieces of research. First, the American sociologist Christian Smith has spent decades researching the faith of American teenagers. What Smith argues is that what parents believe, and how they practice and live out their Christian faith, has huge implications for their children's own faith formation and, crucially, whether their faith will stick.

Secondly, the importance of the family in the transmission of faith has also been recognized by the sociologist Professor Vern L Bengston. In *Families and Faith: How Religion Is Passed Down Across Generations*, Bengston and his co-authors engaged in a longitudinal study in Southern California over a 35-year period on the central question of how faith is transmitted between generations.[40] Interestingly, what they discovered was that whether or not a child continued in the faith they were raised in was determined by the level of intimacy and the closeness of the bond the child had with their father. According to Bengston, 'A father who is an exemplar, a pillar of the church, but doesn't provide warmth and affirmation to his kid does not have

Whether or not a child continued in the faith was determined by the level of intimacy the child had with their father

kids who follow him in his faith.'[41] In other words, this research supports the biblical command, explored in the previous chapter, for fathers to raise their children in the Christian faith but also the need for fathers to be intimately involved in their children's lives in a nurturing and close manner.

Therefore the church must begin to prioritize and take seriously this important task.[42] Churches should begin to encourage fathers, if they are not already doing so, to become involved in family devotions or (if they already are) to better equip them for this task. Fathers should be encouraged to recognize that they are, as Rachel Turner puts it, 'parenting children for a life of faith.'[43] In other words the call of Prov 22.6 to…'train children in the right way, and when old, they will not stray' begins in the home. Parenting children for a lifetime of faith begins in familiar places such as around the kitchen table, in the park or in the car on the way to school. What a privilege fathers have to teach their children how to pray and read the Bible!

Encourage Mentoring and Intergenerational Fathering

An important priority for any church seeking to engage with fathers and fatherhood issues must be to develop a culture where men, across and between the generations, model what it means to be a Christian father, husband and man. Put differently, we might think of this as intergenerational fathering.[44] Boys growing up in the early twenty-first century face unprecedented challenges and must navigate the pressures of a hyper-sexualized world where online games, digital technology, the widespread availability of pornography and social media provide access to information and experiences unknown in previous generations.[45] To help boys navigate these unprecedented pressures they need role models and mentors to help them transition through the various stages, because the boys of today are the fathers and father figures of tomorrow. They need to be surrounded by men—not only their fathers, but ideally a wider church family—who will help them make the transition from boyhood to manhood.

As the late American anthropologist, Margaret Mead puts it, 'The primary task of every civilization is to teach the young men how to be fathers.'[46] Boys need to see male role models in the church from the beginning. That means male volunteers helping in the crèche, Sunday school, parents and toddlers, youth club and other organizations.[47] This also means encouraging the older generation in church to become involved in this process of intergenerational fathering. Older members who belong to a parish church and perhaps think of themselves as having little more to offer should be encouraged to assume the role of father figures to the next generation.

African Bull Elephants—the Need for Male Mentors

Both Angus Buchan[48] and Richard Rohr in their writing share a story that reinforces the need for more mentoring in our churches.[49] In a game reserve in South Africa a group of young bull elephants were causing havoc and killing other animals on the reserve. This puzzled the park rangers who, together with some scientists, began to investigate why this trouble had occurred. Their investigation found that in the reserve there were no older bull elephants. They had either died or been removed by mistake.

Immediately, plans were made to return some of the older bull elephants. To their astonishment, within a few weeks order had been returned to the game reserve. According to Rohr, 'All the old bulls did was wave their ears and make various sounds or small charges, and somehow the younger male elephants understood through these communications that their behaviour was not the way good elephant boys should act…things returned to normal once the elders operated as elders.'[50]

What can be said is this: if it is true of elephants, it is true of men and boys also. In this current generation there is an urgent need for older men to model to boys and young adults what it means to be a Christlike father and husband. As the apostle Paul said to the Corinthian church: 'For though you might have ten thousand guardians in Christ, you do not have many fathers' (1 Cor 4.15). We need more fathers.

Rites of Passage

The former teacher turned popular author, Sue Palmer, in her book *21st Century Boys,* writes that 'Boys need quests to pursue, codes to live by and mentors to guide them.'[51] It would appear that this author, writing from a non-faith perspective, has described exactly what the Christian faith can offer through the local church.[52] One of the key ways in which intergenerational fathering can be encouraged and developed is through greater engagement by churches with rites of passage. Rites of passage and Christian initiation are interwoven with church life. Indeed, the Anglican church itself is already involved in a range of liturgically grounded rites of passage. Rites of passage are inescapable and serve to mark an individual's transition and movement between generations or in their role within the family and in wider society.

However, as Ronald L Grimes argues, North American culture, and, arguably, Western culture in general, has become ritually impoverished, lacking any notion of rites of passage and transition from different phases of life.[53] This ritual impoverishment is particularly striking when it comes to manhood and boys becoming men. For Richard Rohr, this lack of 'patterns of initiation'[54] lies 'at the heart of many of our cultural and religious problems today.'[55] Boys have no idea when they become men and in the absence of proper patterns and rituals of initiation, resort instead to destructive rites of passage that damage themselves and those around them. Therefore the local church could take the lead in encouraging fathers, parents and families to take seriously the stages in their children's lives and help them to prepare appropriate rites of passage for boys moving to adulthood.[56]

Fatherlessness

In a previous chapter we identified and discussed the growing social trend towards fatherlessness within contemporary society and the reality that significant numbers of young children are growing up without a father at home. The scale of father absence within society is a social reality that the church cannot afford to ignore. The church has a pastoral priority to engage with fatherless children within society. There are some examples within the Church of Ireland of this happening. Indeed, it is worth drawing attention to one such initiative, which might work in other parts of the church. Muckamore Parish Church (St Jude's) outside Antrim in the Diocese of Connor is one such church.

The church has a pastoral priority to engage with fatherless children within society

What Muckamore Parish Did

- Recognized that many children in a school within their parish had absent fathers.
- Started a programme called 'Boys to Men' to provide boys aged 10 and 11 lacking a father figure in their life with some practical life skills.
- Activities included teaching boys how to wire a plug, some basic cookery skills, how to polish shoes and polish a car.
- Started with boys but then also expanded to include girls who also lacked a father figure in their lives.
- There were also opportunities to use the sessions to explore more about the Christian faith.
- Encouraged men and women in the parish to share some of their own practical skills with the boys and girls.

Calling God Father

The reality of human sin and brokenness means that fathers will make mistakes. Sometimes these mistakes have caused untold hurt to children. Many people, both within the church and outside it, have endured profound suffering because of an abusive, apathetic or absent father. It is only by the grace of God that those people could ever believe that God as Father means something different. As we have established, God's fatherhood functions as the standard against which all human fatherhood, good and bad, is measured. Moreover, because of that, it does not matter if one experienced the best or worst of human fatherhood, because God's fatherhood is so utterly different and better than even the best of earthly fathers. At the heart of the Christian faith is the generous, abundant and compassionate love of God the Father. Pastorally and missionally, the proclamation of the love of the Father matters for each and every person in society.

Evangelism

The priority of the Christian church, through the Great Commission, must be to proclaim the love of the Father as revealed through his Son's death on the cross. Therefore, the proclamation of the kingdom of God and the Son's revelation of the Father are intimately connected. At the heart of the Christian faith is the truth that on the cross Christ came to reveal the Father's love. This Father is beyond all human comprehension. One of the most profound missional and pastoral challenges the church faces is engaging with men in the UK who, according to a number of statistical sources, do not go to church on a regular basis. A further section of society also missing from the church is the so-called millennial generation—those in their 20s and 30s born between the early 1980s and the turn of the millennium. One could argue that millennial fathers might be the hardest for the church to engage with, given that both men and millennials are largely absent from our churches. However, this is where engaging in fatherhood issues could provide the church with a mission opportunity to reach out to these millennial dads who, as chapter two demonstrated, are more likely to want to be involved in their children's lives.

Ideas for Working with Dads

Dads and Toddlers

Some churches run a 'dads and toddlers morning' on Saturdays. This could be based on the very successful 'Who Let the Dads Out' programme or could be marketed differently, such as 'Mum's Lie-in.'[57] Whatever you call it, the most important thing is gathering men together with their young children. Usually, some sort of breakfast is involved, along with toys for the children to play with. How you run it is up to you. Simply find a space and a group of young dads who share your passion to work with dads in the local community.

Dads and Daughters/Lads and Dads/Dads and Children Events

There is the possibility of running events specifically for dads and daughters, such as an all-age Sunday afternoon with a picnic and games.[58] Equally, for boys, why not run a lads and dads football competition or sports event? You could also organize a 'men up a mountain' afternoon for fathers with their children.

Fatherhood Courses

There are a number of courses on fatherhood devised by Care for the Family called 'Time Out for Dads.'[59] The course consists of four sessions, which focus on the importance of fathers and help you to build a positive relationship with your children. The course includes sessions looking at what dads are for, as well as love, training and discipline, with optional sessions on stepfamilies. The 'Daddy Cool Parenting Course' is a free, five-session course with full instructions on the 'Who Let the Dads Out' website.[60]

'Dadfest' and Special Father's Day's Service

Large churches such as Willow Creek Community Church in Chicago and the Causeway Coast Vineyard Church in Coleraine, Northern Ireland run very successful events called 'Dadfest' on Father's Day weekend. Essentially they are a festival celebrating fathers and father figures with things of interest to men. This can include a classic car display, BBQ, sports, outdoor games and competitions. It is a great idea for outreach into the community, as it allows you the opportunity to invite families to a special Father's Day celebration on the Sunday, if you hold the event on the Saturday. Why not consider running this as a church or together with other local churches in your community?

Ideas for Supporting New Dads in the Church

- Run a 'Let's Stick Together Course' (by Care for the Family) aimed at new parents.[61]
- As part of the baptism process, either before or during the service present each father with a copy of *The Sixty Minute Father* by Rob Parsons.[62]
- When a new baby is born, organize for someone from church to provide some babysitting, to allow the mum and dad to go out for coffee or dinner.
- Assign parental mentors to come alongside new parents to encourage and help them.
- Buy new dads a 'Dad-to-be' survival kit with some fun, novelty presents. In addition to this the church could include a Bible, or

another men's devotional book. You could also add a children's or beginner's Bible or another age-appropriate children's Bible story book, to encourage the dad to start early in passing on faith.

Men's Bible Study on Fatherhood Through the Movies

Introduce a men's Bible study on fatherhood through the lens of some famous movies about fatherhood such as the *The Pursuit of Happyness; Finding Nemo; Father of the Bride; Courageous; Boyz N the Hood; To Kill a Mockingbird; Unconditional* and *Taken.* Each time you meet, explore the ideas and themes about fatherhood that emerge from these movies and how they connect with biblical principles on fathering, such as dedication, commitment, self-sacrifice, seeking the lost and passing on faith.

Working with the Fatherless

Why not approach your local school to see if fathers or retired men can help with after-school homework clubs (safeguarding checks will be required).

As a church, take part in Orphan Sunday and encourage parishioners to consider registering with the statutory agencies to adopt or foster.

Equally, register your church as a 'Home for Good' church and become a local champion for fostering and adoption in your area.[63]

Notes

1 J I Packer, *Knowing God* (London: Hodder and Stoughton, 1973) p 224.

2 K J Vanhoozer (ed), *Everyday Theology* (Grand Rapids, MI: Baker, 2007) p 55.

3 This is the most up-to-date data available from the Office for National Statistics (ONS) for 2015 released on 5 November: http://www.ons.gov.uk/ons/publications/re-reference-tables.html?edition=tcm%3A77-401852

4 http://www.ons.gov.uk/ons/rel/family-demography/families-and-households/2011/sum-lone-parents.html

5 Centre for Social Justice, *Fractured Families: Why Stability Matters* (London: Centre for Social Justice, 2013) available at: http://www.centreforsocialjustice.org.uk/UserStorage/pdf/Pdf%20reports/CSJ_Fractured_Families_Report_WEB_13.06.13.pdf

6 http://www.fatherhoodinstitute.org/about-the-fatherhood-institute/

7 The Fatherhood Institute, *Addressing Fatherlessness: how Government can strengthen the active presence of fathers in their children's lives* (London: The Fatherhood Institute, 2012).

8 Centre for Social Justice, *Fully Committed: How government could reverse family breakdown* (London: Centre for Social Justice, 2014) available at: http://www.centreforsocialjustice.org.uk/UserStorage/pdf/Pdf%20reports/CSJJ2072_Family_Breakdown.pdf p 23.

9 Centre for Social Justice, *Fully Committed, op cit,* p 27.

10 J McGregor, 'How Mark Zuckerberg changed the face of fatherhood,' *The Age*, 27 November 2015: http://www.theage.com.au/comment/facebooks-mark-zuckerberg-plans-to-ditch-rat-race-for-stroller-circuit-on-paternity-leave-20151126-gl9gnp.html

11 E Dermott, *Intimate Fatherhood: A Sociological Analysis* (Abingdon: Routledge, 2008) p 7.

12 E Dermott and T Miller, 'More than the sum of its parts? Contemporary fatherhood policy, practice and discourse,' *Families, Relationships and Societies* vol 4, no 2, 183–195 (2013) p 183.

13 T Miller, *'Making Sense of Fatherhood: Gender, Caring and Work'* (Cambridge University Press, 2011) p 1.

14 Working Families, *Modern Families Index 2016* (London: Working Families, 2016). Available at: http://www.workingfamilies.org.uk/wp-content/uploads/2016/02/Modern-Families-Index-2016.pdf

15 Church of Ireland, *Book of Common Prayer* (Dublin: Columba Press, 2004) p 205.

16 M M Thompson, *The Promise of the Father: Jesus and God in the New Testament* (Louisville, KY: Westminster John Knox Press, 2000).

17 W Brueggemann, *Isaiah 1–39: A Commentary* (Louisville, KY: Westminster John Knox Press, 1998) p 19.

18 T Smail, *The Forgotten Father* (London: Wipf and Stock, 2001) p 52.

19 E Brunner, *Dogmatics I: The Christian Doctrine of God* (trans Olive Wyon) (London: Lutterworth Press, 1949) p 206.

20 K E Bailey, *Jesus Through Middle Eastern Eyes: Cultural Studies in the Gospels* (London: SPCK, 2008) p 96.

21 J Ratzinger, *The God of Jesus Christ: Meditations on the Triune God* (San Francisco: Ignatius Press, 2008) p 33.

22 K Barth, *Church Dogmatics Study Edition 2: The Doctrine of the Word of God I.1 § 8–12* (London and New York: Continuum International Publishing Group, 2004) p 389.

23 J Stott, *The Message of Ephesians* (Nottingham: IVP, 1989) p 134.

24 W Brueggemann, *Old Testament Theology* (Nashville, TN: Abingdon Press, 2008) p 115.

25 K E Bailey, *Jesus Through Middle Eastern Eyes, op cit*, p 99.

26 K E Bailey, *Finding the Lost Cultural Keys to Luke 15* (St Louis, MO: Concordia Publishing House, 1992) p 191.

27 N T Wright, *Jesus and the Victory of God* (London: SPCK, 1996) pp 129–135.

28 K E Bailey, *Finding the Lost Cultural Keys to Luke 15, op cit*, pp 143–144.

29 K E Bailey, *Finding the Lost Cultural Keys to Luke 15, op cit*, p 144.

30 K E Bailey, *Finding the Lost Cultural Keys to Luke 15, op cit*, p 172.

31 Dionysius of Halicarnassus (Rom Ant 2.26.4) as quoted in A T Lincoln, *Ephesians* (Dallas, TX: Word Books, 1990) p 398.

32 P T O'Brien,*The Letter to the Ephesians: The Pillar New Testament Commentary* (Grand Rapids, MI: Eerdmans, 1999) p 447.

33 Douglas Moo, *The Letters to the Colossians and to Philemon: The Pillar New Testament Commentary* (Grand Rapids, MI: Eerdmans, 2008) p 307.

34 A T Lincoln, *Ephesians* (Dallas, TX: Word Books, 1990) p 406.

35 A T Lincoln, *Ephesians, op cit*, p 407.

36 A T Lincoln, *Ephesians, op cit*, p 407.

37 C J H Wright, 'Family,' in David Noel Freedman (ed), *The Anchor Bible Dictionary Vol 2 D–G* (New York: Doubleday, 1992) p 764.

38 C J H Wright, 'Family,' *op cit*, p 765.

39 C Smith, *Souls in Transition: The Religious and Spiritual Lives of Emerging Adults* (Oxford University Press, 2009) and Christian Smith, *Soul Searching: the Religious and Spiritual Lives of American Teenagers* (Oxford University Press, 2005).

40 V L Bengston, N M Putney and S Harris, *Families and Faith: How Religion is Passed Down Across Generations* (Oxford University Press, 2013).

41 http://www.nytimes.com/2014/02/01/us/book-explores-ways-faith-is-kept-or-lost-over-generations.html?_r=3

42 The Church of Ireland has already recognized the importance of the family in the intergenerational transmission of Christian faith. In 2012 it launched *Family Time*—a resource aimed at helping parents and the wider family circle: http://familyfaith.co.uk

43 R Turner, *Parenting Children for a Life of Faith* (Abingdon: Bible Reading Fellowship, 2010).

44 C L Ross and H C Allen, *Intergenerational Christian Formation: Bringing the Whole Church Together in Ministry, Community and Worship* (Downer's Grove, Il: IVP Academic, 2012).

45 For further on this please see Philip Zimbardo and Nikita D Coulombe, *Man Disconnected: How Technology Has Sabotaged What it Means to be Male* (London: Penguin, Random House, 2015).

46 As quoted in D Eberly, *Faith Factor in Fatherhood* (Lanham, MD: Lexington, 1999) p 5.

47 For more on this see: N Harding, *Boys, God and the Church: How Churches Can Help Boys Grow in Faith and Why They Do Not!* (Grove Pastoral booklet P111).

48 A Buchan, *Fathers and Sons: Building a Strong and God-honoring Relationship* (Vereeniging, South Africa: Christian Art Publishers, 2015).

49 R Rohr, *Adam's Return: The Five Promises of Male Initiation* (New York: Crossroad Publishing Company, 2004) pp 11–12.

50 R Rohr, *Adam's Return, op cit,* p 12.

51 S Palmer, *Twenty-first century Boys: How modern life is driving them off the rails and how we can get them back on track* (London: Orion Books, 2009) p 260.

52 This could also be achieved in partnership with other organizations such as the Boys' Brigade, whose stated objective is: 'The advancement of Christ's kingdom among Boys and the promotion of habits of Obedience, Reverence, Discipline, Self-respect and all that tends towards a true Christian manliness.' http://boys-brigade.org.uk/who-we-are/

53 R L Grimes, *'Deeply Into the Bone: Re-inventing Rites of Passage'* (California: University of California Press, 2002).

54 R Rohr, *Adam's Return, op cit,* p 2.

55 R Rohr, *Adam's Return, op cit,* p 2.

56 For more on this please see Stu Webber, *Tender Warrior: God's Intention for a Man* (Colorado Springs, CO: Multnomah Books, 1993) pp 155–169.

57 https://www.wholetthedadsout.org.uk

58 Please see additional material online for a running order for such an event.

59 http://www.careforthefamily.org.uk/time-out-for-dads-parenting-course

60 http://www.wholetthedadsout.org.uk/running-group/daddy-cool-parenting-course

61 http://www.careforthefamily.org.uk/courses-lets-stick-together

62 R Parsons, *The Sixty Minute Father* (London: Hodder and Stoughton, 1995).

63 http://www.homeforgood.org.uk/get-involved/churches